THE GREENE COUNTY MUSEUM:
HISTORY THROUGH THE EYES OF A CHILD

Anita Rowe Stafford

Published by Laughing Ladybug Press

THE GREENE COUNTY MUSEUM:
HISTORY THROUGH THE EYES OF A CHILD

First edition. August 24, 2022.

Written by Anita Rowe Stafford.

This book is dedicated to those individuals who have
preserved the history of Greene County, Arkansas,
so that the past may never be forgotten.

This is the Greene County Museum in Paragould, Arkansas. The museum is a place where both children and adults can visit to learn about the history of Northeast Arkansas.

Today a school group will be touring the museum, and one student is especially excited. JJ heard that the museum has displays of artifacts and relics from the past.

JJ stepped inside and looked around. He spotted a photograph of a man above the fireplace mantel.

Photo: University of Arkansas 1935 Razorback

The tour guide said this photograph is former Arkansas Governor J. Marion Futrell. The museum building was the home of Governor Futrell and his family during the early 1900s.

This room contains several items from the time the Futrell family lived in the house. JJ heard the tour guide say that this chair once belonged to Governor Futrell.

When the tour moved to the next room, JJ learned that the first people to live in Northeast Arkansas were Native Americans. The Shawnee lived in the area of Greene County we now call Walcott. The Delaware tribe inhabited the forests and streams of Delaplaine, and the Osage flourished in both Lafe and Lorado.

Long ago, Native Americans used *Signal Trees* to mark routes. Trail marker trees were bent and shaped while young. These trees are now hundreds of years old. JJ thinks a tree like this one would be an exciting find in the forest.

Signal trees are not the only relics Native Americans left behind in Northeast Arkansas. The museum also has displays of other artifacts, such as this arrowhead collection.

Each of these carved rocks served a special purpose. Some were for hunting and others were used as tools.

Benjamin Crowley came as the first settler to this area of the Arkansas Territory in 1821. This photograph shows a replica of the Crowley house. His settlement became known as Crowley's Ridge. He found his neighbors, the Shawnee, to be peaceful and helpful people. After more settlers arrived, Greene County was formed and was named for Revolutionary War General Nathanael Greene. Arkansas became the 25th state in 1836.

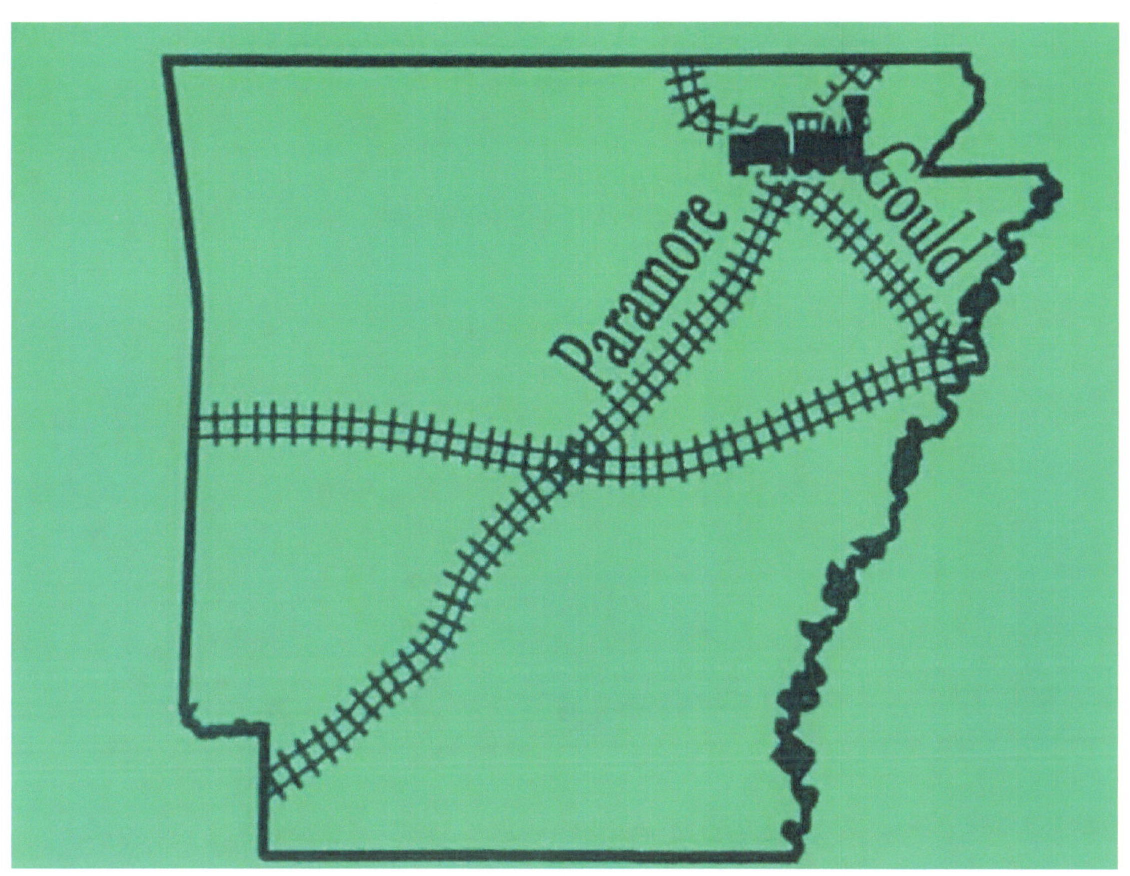

During the 1880s Jay Gould and J. W. Paramore built railroads across Arkansas. The railroads crossed in the northeast corner of the state. This is where the city of Paragould was born in 1883. Along with the railroad came business and industry, and Paragould soon grew into a modern city.

The Greene County Courthouse was built in Paragould in 1888. The four-faced clock dome sat atop the building until 1968, when it was removed for safety reasons. Later, when the courthouse was restored, the old clock tower was replaced.

Here, JJ gets a close-up look at one of the original clock faces that once crowned the roof of the Greene County Courthouse.

Before textile factories, our ancestors used spinning wheels to make their own yarn from raw cotton. JJ has seen cotton growing in the field, but he has never seen one of these spinning wheels used to make yarn.

14

JJ toured a kitchen from a century ago. At that time homemakers baked their own bread and prepared food on stoves heated by wood.

Doing the family laundry must have taken a lot longer before automatic washing machines were invented. JJ has never seen laundry equipment quite like this.

The museum tour gave JJ glimpses of some early communication devices, like this large, wooden telephone. He noticed how different it is from the phones his family uses. No one could carry this phone in a pocket.

JJ saw this advertisement sign display for a lumber company from many years ago. He noticed that the telephone number was only two digits. How many digits are in your telephone number?

Another display at the museum is of an old school room. JJ was able to get a close-up look at the kind of school his ancestors attended. At one time, there were more than 50 small schools located in the different communities throughout Greene County.

Next, the school group climbed the tall stairs to get a look at the rest of the museum. JJ could see the street below from the second story window.

This is where JJ found the Military Room. He saw military uniforms and equipment used by soldiers from Greene County in all the wars. He saw a photograph of Veterans from the Civil War and a bugle from World War I.

JJ found more artifacts on the outside of the museum. He did not expect to see a horse trough from 1878. This trough stood in front of the county courthouse in Gainesville and once held water for horses to drink while their owners had business inside.

22

JJ also explored an old water fountain in front of the museum. Four fountains like this one served downtown Paragould during the mid-1900s. The reputation of the fountains was that they dispensed hot water during warm months or remained frozen during cold weather.

JJ learned all about the history of Northeast Arkansas, and now he recommends that YOU visit the Greene County Museum, too.

Also by Anita Stafford

Picture books
A Vegetable Garden is Not For Cows
Briley Isabelle Gordon Wants a Cat
The Disappearance of Mr. White
Vegetables Smegetables
Hooray Hooray It's Purple Day
We Are Different, We Are the Same
Laughing Ladybug Meets the Grumpy Bugs
If Moms Were Flowers I'd Pick You
Can You See Me Now: Cheetahs Hiding in Plain Sight
The Squirrel School Picnic
My Brother's Allergy: Peanuts

The Career Kids Series
Uncle Philip is a Farmer
Aunt Tiffany is an Artist
Aunt Virginia is a Seamstress
Aunt Kelly is a Realtor
Uncle Daniel is a Systems Engineer

Chapter books
The Sassafras House series including:
The Legend of Sassafras House
Treasure in Catclaw Canyon
The Catnapper Mystery

For adults
Confessions of a Cell Phone Loser

Watch for more at https://www.anitastafford.com

About the Author

Anita Rowe Stafford makes her home in northeastern Arkansas. She worked in public school for more than twenty years as a teacher and a counselor. Anita has taught students from kindergarten to graduate level, and she is also a Licensed Professional Counselor.

The Greene County Museum is located at 130 South 14th Street in Paragould, Arkansas. The museum is a nonprofit organization and depends on community support and volunteers. Annual, business, and lifetime memberships are available. Monetary donations are always appreciated.

"Preserving the past for the future."